America's Kitchen

America's Kitchen

Traditional & Contemporary Regional Cooking

featuring recipes from

America's Most Celebrated Chefs

Anthony Dias Blue

Photography by Joyce Oudkerk Pool
Recipes developed by Kathryn Blue and Diana Torrey

Turner Publishing, Inc.
ATLANTA

To America's regional cooks,
who have carefully preserved and enriched our heritage
and ourselves.

Copyright © 1995 by Anthony Dias Blue
Recipe photographs copyright © 1995 by Joyce Oudkerk Pool
Illustrations copyright © 1995 by Rick Powell

Library of Congress Cataloging-in-Publication Data
Blue, Anthony Dias.
    America's kitchen: traditional and contemporary regional cooking featuring recipes from
America's most celebrated chefs / Anthony Dias Blue; photography by Joyce Oudkerk Pool. —1st ed.
      p. cm.
   ISBN 1-57036-161-4 (alk. paper)
   1. Cookery, American. I Title.
     TX715.D57 1995
      641.5973—dc20   95-10800
                                             CIP

Karen E. Smith, Book Design and Art Direction
Stephanie Greenleigh, Diana Torrey, Food Stylists
Carol Hacker, Prop Stylist
Claudia Breault, Assistant Food Stylist
Carmen Alvarez, Photography Assistant
J. Stoll, Silhouette Photography

Published by Turner Publishing, Inc.
A Subsidiary of Turner Broadcasting System, Inc.
1050 Techwood Drive, N.W.
Atlanta, Georgia 30318

Distributed by Andrews and McMeel
A Universal Press Syndicate Company
4900 Main Street
St. Louis, Missouri 64112

First Edition
10 9 8 7 6 5 4 3 2 1

Printed in Italy

Contents

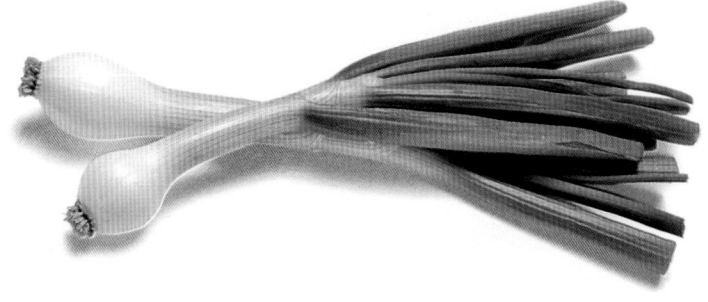

Introduction

There is no American Cuisine.

How do you reconcile clam chowder and *huevos rancheros,* or seared ahi and Brunswick stew? The answer is: you don't. America is too big, too diverse, too complex to have a single cuisine; instead, it has many.

What is a "cuisine" anyway? Simply put, it is a style of cooking based on a locally grown pantry of ingredients and a unique set of cultural influences. It is affected by geography, timing, and people. The United States is vast enough to hold all of western Europe and a goodly chunk of Asia, and just as these regions have produced a multitude of cuisines, so has America.

But how do we divide the country into its component cuisines? Does the food of Dallas differ greatly from the food of Houston? Is San Francisco cooking significantly distinct from Los Angeles cooking? Each place, each city, each village in America has culinary influences in unique combination. The local farms, the economic level of the inhabitants, the cultural and ethnic backgrounds that they bring to bear—all affect the dishes created in local kitchens. Although the food in Dallas is somewhat different from the food in Houston or Santa Fe or Phoenix, there are regional factors and cultural similarities that tie these places together. There is much more of an affinity among these Southwest cities than there is between Dallas and, say, Boston.

The defining aspect of a regional cuisine is the pantry of ingredients available to and used by local cooks. Corn in the South, New England, and the Heartland; salmon in the Northwest; salad greens in California; chiles in the Southwest—these are the building blocks of America's regional cuisines.

Although specific items may cross regional boundaries, each of the nine disciplines presented here has at its heart an individualized palette of ingredients.

The factors that combine to create these regional pantries have as much to do with environmental influences as cultural ones. The climate of Florida makes citrus fruit an important ingredient in that region; the soil in California's San Joaquin Valley makes almonds and walnuts key elements of that region's cuisine; proximity to the sea has great impact in Hawaii, California, the Northwest, Florida, and New England. But, most important of all, perhaps, are the cultural traditions brought by the people who settled in each region.

Spain helped shape cooking in the Southwest, New Orleans, and California, while England influenced New England and the South. As time passed, cultural influences kept being added in all the regions. In the South, African ingredients and culture were augmented later by Italian and French cooking traditions; in the Southwest, Native American traditions were blended with Spanish; Hawaii was shaped by Polynesian, then European, and, more recently, Japanese cultures.

Nine distinct American cuisines have emerged—some early in the history of the nation, others much later—and each as complex and varied as the cuisine of a European or Asian nation. But appreciation of these American regional cuisines was not automatic. Most Americans didn't even know they existed. For most of the twentieth century "American food" was regarded as bland, homogenized, and unimaginative meat-and-potatoes fare. Overcooked roasts, chicken à la king, hot dogs, sandwiches on Wonder bread, tuna casserole, and Jell-O molds were typical home cooking. Special events were celebrated at overly fancy and intimidating restaurants that served such grandiose "continental" dishes as Beef Wellington and Veal Prince Orloff.

A revolution began in 1961 with the publication of *Mastering the Art of French Cooking* by Simone Beck, Louisette Bertholle, and Julia Child. This book, along with Ms. Child's television cooking show, convinced Americans that cooking could be fun and the end result could be extraordinarily pleasing. Suddenly, *coq au vin* and *boeuf Bourguignon* had replaced the dreary food of the 1950s. For the next decade or so, Americans went on a binge of cooking and eating—but the subject of their affection was not American food.

First it was French food, then Italian. Soon enough Americans had bought woks and were producing *moo goo gai pan* at home. They made a culinary world tour at their kitchen stoves. This was a necessary step, as American cooks needed to familiarize themselves with classic cuisines in order to appreciate their own. They needed to learn the traditional techniques and concepts that were so influential on indigenous cooking styles.

When food became a passion among Americans, it was only a matter of time before the nation rediscovered its own culinary heritage. With the help of dedicated cooks such as Paul Prudhomme, Wolfgang Puck, Jeremiah Tower, Mark Miller, and many others who contributed their own interpretation of the established regional cooking traditions, the greatness of American regional cuisine was revealed.

America's Kitchen celebrates our nine indigenous regional cuisines. The foods represented here explore both their traditional and contemporary interpretations and are extraordinarily delicious. They also reaffirm what Dorothy discovered on her long journey to Oz: There's no place like home.

AMERICA'S CULINARY REGIONS

- New England
- The South
- Florida
- New Orleans
- The Heartland
- The Northwest
- The Southwest
- California
- Hawaii

New England

When the Pilgrims, weary and battered from their North Atlantic crossing, stumbled ashore on the rocky coast of America in 1620, they brought with them fervent fundamentalist ideas about religion and some equally strong beliefs about food. Led by Miles Standish, the company of more than one hundred men and women established their settlement at Plymouth, Massachusetts, an abandoned Indian village surrounded by barren land and besieged by hostile weather. During the first winter and the months that followed, half of the Pilgrims died, and those who weren't claimed by disease and the harsh conditions nearly starved to death.

The Puritan Food Ethic

Ironically, these first New Englanders were surrounded by an abundance of food sources, but their inflexibility—a characteristic of their religious beliefs —carried over into most other aspects of their lives, including the foods they ate. At least at the beginning, they rejected much of the native foodstuffs. Lobsters of enormous size, for example, were so plentiful that after particularly violent storms, deep piles of them washed up on the beaches and were left to rot by settlers who considered them peasant food and refused to eat them.

The settlers were singularly ill-equipped for their new environment. They were not skilled at farming or hunting, and fishing was foreign to them. If it had not been for the remarkably friendly local tribes, the Pilgrims would have perished. The Native American tribes—Algonquin, Mohegan, Narraganset, and Penobscot—taught them how to survive in their newly adopted home.

The settlers learned and mastered the techniques for planting corn and beans, as well as pumpkins and other squash. The newcomers also learned to gather clams at low tide, and they learned the native technique for building a clambake (see page 24).

Corn to the Rescue

It was corn, however, that saved the Pilgrims from starvation and helped establish Massachusetts. A cache of corn, discovered by Miles Standish, helped many of the pioneers survive the hard first winter. In the spring, after the ground began to thaw, the survivors planted crude corn fields. The settlers were taught to pulverize the corn kernels into a primitive meal called samp. From this basic ingredient they sifted out the fine cornmeal and made a mush that was called "hasty pudding." They also mixed this cornmeal with scalded milk and made baked or fried biscuits called "Johnny cakes." These dense, almost indestructible cakes traveled well and allowed the Pilgrims to venture farther from home for hunting and gathering food.

One basic dish that the settlers adopted almost immediately from the Native American diet was succotash, made by adding beans to cooked corn or cornmeal mush. This dish became a year-round staple. In the summer it was made from fresh ingredients, and in the winter from dried beans and samp.

The Pantry Takes Shape

The introduction of basic farming expanded and balanced the New England diet, and in 1624 the first cattle arrived. This event was significant for a number of reasons: dairy products and meat became a regular part of the diet, and strong backs were now available to pull plows. By 1640 most of the ingredients for the emerging regional cuisine were established. The settlers, joined by thousands of new arrivals, were already turning out chowders, stews, boiled beef, and fruit pies.

The larder of New World ingredients determined the character of this new cuisine. Corn, beans, pumpkins, squash, cranberries, blueberries, wild turkeys, steamer clams, quahogs, sugar maples, and, yes, lobsters defined the food New Englanders ate. Wheat and rye took on importance once livestock was available to till the fields. Many other ingredients were imported. Apple orchards, for example, were planted from seedlings brought from Europe, the first of which arrived in 1629. Chickens were imported, as were pigs. Salt spray roses, the source of rose hips used for jelly, were imported from China in the early 1800s.

Eventually settlers arrived who understood fishing. Coming mainly from Italy and Portugal (particularly the Azores), these hardy souls discovered the vast resources of Georges Bank, an enormous underwater plateau southeast of Boston that is the richest fishing area off the east coast of North America. They found cod, hake, pollock, haddock, monkfish, mackerel, smelt, bluefish, butterfish, and shad.

The One-Pot Kitchen

The cuisine was defined by its ingredients and shaped by the iron cooking pot. Each New England home revolved around the hearth. Especially in winter and during the many cool days of fall and spring, this area of the house was where people gathered to warm themselves. The glowing coals of the big stone fireplace burned from morning until night. Hanging over the fire was a large cast-iron pot in which the day's meal would be bubbling and stewing. On any given day there might be chicken in the pot, or ham, or codfish. Whatever the protein, there were always vegetables, either fresh or dried or preserved and put up the previous summer and fall.

At dinner time, the heavy pot was hauled to the nearby table where the family gathered. The one-dish stew was ladled into wooden bowls and eaten as the family conversed about the happenings of the day. The pot became a portable heater and a center of conversation as well as a provider of sustenance. Such New England traditions as boiled dinner and baked beans are direct descendants of the one-pot cooking style.

Economic Development

In addition to native crops, the colonists also raised vegetables brought from England. Cabbages, leeks, onions, and turnips were widely planted. Among fruits, apple, apricot, plum, and pear trees flourished.

Missing their customary pint of English ale, the settlers were quick to import wheat, barley, and hops. By 1640 a brewery was already established and licensed, and even the strictest Puritans began their day with ale or beer. But wheat and barley did not thrive in the rocky soil, and thirsty colonials turned to wines made from mulberries, cherries, and dandelion blossoms and to the abundant apple orchards. Hard cider became the beverage of choice.

By the end of the seventeenth century a new rival for cider had appeared. Growing shipping trade brought molasses, the by-product of sugar plantations in the West Indies. This thick, black syrup wasn't needed for sweetening—the area produced plenty of maple sugar for that purpose. (One important exception to this were baked beans, which were traditionally sweetened with molasses.) The vast majority of the molasses brought to New England was distilled into rum.

Other boats in the waters of the North Atlantic plied a different trade. Hardy fishermen brought loads of fresh seafood to the tables of New Englanders. The harsh climate and the abundance of fish and shellfish made seafood more important in the cuisine of New England than it was in any other region. Fishing was basic to the economy, and clams, oysters, and scallops were basic ingredients on regional tables. Oh yes, and lobster finally took its rightful place as the king of shellfish.

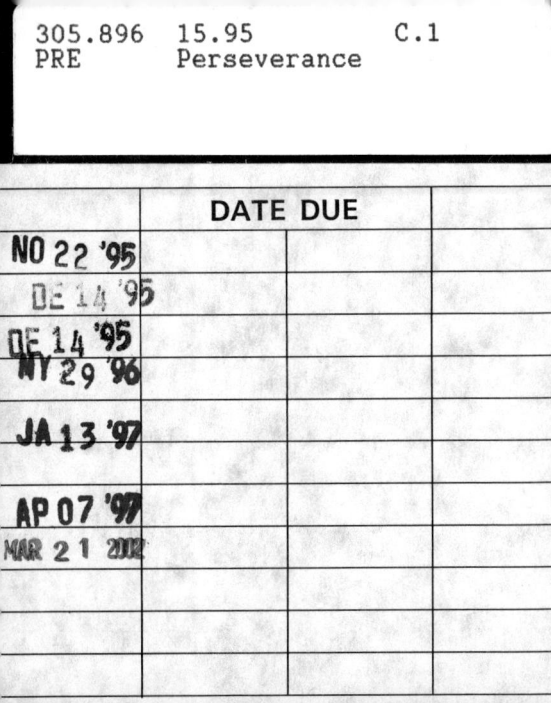